CHAPPELL ROAN

The Ultimate Unofficial Midwest Princess Fan Book

Natty Kasambala

HarperCollins*Publishers*

HarperCollins*Publishers*
1 London Bridge Street
London SE1 9GF

www.harpercollins.co.uk

HarperCollins*Publishers*
Macken House, 39/40 Mayor Street Upper
Dublin 1, D01 C9W8, Ireland

First published by HarperCollins*Publishers* 2025

10 9 8 7 6 5 4 3 2 1

Text © HarperCollins*Publishers* 2025

Natty Kasambala asserts the moral right to be identified as the author of this work

A catalogue record of this book is available from the British Library

ISBN 978-0-00-875766-3

Printed and bound by PNB, Latvia

All rights reserved. No part of this publication may be reproduced, stored in a retrieval system, or transmitted, in any form or by any means, electronic, mechanical, photocopying, recording or otherwise, without the prior written permission of the publishers.

Without limiting the author's and publisher's exclusive rights, any unauthorised use of this publication to train generative artificial intelligence (AI) technologies is expressly prohibited. HarperCollins also exercise their rights under Article 4(3) of the Digital Single Market Directive 2019/790 and expressly reserve this publication from the text and data mining exception.

This book is produced from FSC™ certified paper and other controlled sources to ensure responsible forest management.

For more information visit: www.harpercollins.co.uk/green

This work has not been officially endorsed by Chappell Roan, but pays homage to the multi-talented icon that she is. Written by a fan, for fans, it is a tribute to Chappell and everybody she inspires.

CONTENTS

INTRODUCTION
7

10 YEARS IN
THE MAKING
15

MIDWEST
PRINCESS
29

PINK PONY
CLUB
39

HOW TO BE
AUTHENTICALLY YOU
47

LOVER GWORL
57

CAMP ROAN! HER
STYLE EVOLUTION
71

LET'S TALK ABOUT
BOUNDARIES
85

A PHENOMENON
OF THE FEMME VARIETY
97

ACTIVISM &
COMMUNITY
107

JOURNALLING
115

QUIZ TIME
125

RESOURCES
141

PICTURE CREDITS
144

INTRODUCTION

Everyone who's anyone is shouting about Chappell Roan. Her name and her iconic lyrics are on everybody's lips. From sparking spicy discourse about fandoms to instant karaoke classics, the Missouri-born singer has set the pop world alight with her fiercely gilded songwriting pen.

For the uninitiated, here's how you know you've encountered a true Chappell Roan original. Firstly, her earworm melodies will have you humming along before you even think you know the song. Next, you'll feel the sparkly haze of her synth-pop production wash over you like an 1980s fog machine. And when the final layer of her razor-sharp wit hits, you'll be catapulted right back to the present day, entertained by unmistakably modern tales of unrequited love and situationships galore. Her music is a lethal blend of old and new, familiar and yet deeply original, wistful but biting, and it's no wonder that it's captured attention across generations.

And while her pen wears its heart on its sleeve, it's important to emphasise that Roan rarely ever plays victim. Oh no. Her stories are sharpened with a sarcastic edge, rebellious spirit and very occasional full-on revenge fantasies that whip you up into a frenzy right alongside her. Visually, she's just as singular. Adorned to the nines with drag couture and a kaleidoscope of colours and costumes, she's as much a feast for the eyes as the ears. Her bold embrace of pageantry, queerness and musical hooks that simply refuse to leave your brain explain why she's already being dubbed a 'queer pop icon' by many after years in the relative shadows.

Accolades have already started showering down on her. After touring with Olivia Rodrigo, attention turned to her back catalogue, with a VMA and a Grammy for Best New Artist under her belt. There was a point in time, almost a year after her album's release, when Chappell had six songs in the *Billboard* Hot 100 and three in the Top 40 charts at the same time. The craze has been synchronised and unprecedented. Her *first ever* festival performance was in a rammed tent at Coachella, with every minute being clipped and going viral on socials within the day. When she performed at Lollapalooza, her set had to be upgraded to the main stage and the crowd is estimated to have been the largest of all time at the festival, according to their team. And it's not just her project that rocketed off. She followed up the hype in April of 2024 with her first single in the limelight, 'Good Luck, Babe!', to roaring appetite and it hit 1 billion streams on Spotify alone in under six months. There's no doubt that she's a pop phenomenon of the femme variety – she even has a song about it.

For many of us, Chappell's ascent to stardom feels like it happened almost overnight, as if you, and your favourite artist, gained the same favourite artist in an instant. But in reality, the road to success for Miss Roan was 10 years and a lifetime in the making. Signed for the first time as a 17-year-old, Chappell was originally discovered via the covers she posted on YouTube for a few years. Picking up piano from age 10 or 11, she'd been inspired to upload to the platform after winning her school talent show at 13 and dabbling in songwriting at summer camps. It was an original track she'd written there that caught the attention of the music industry and planted the first seeds for the young Missourian that this was a path worth exploring. She showcased at a few labels and eventually landed on Atlantic Records. Moving to LA off the back of the record deal, Roan bounced back and forth between the Californian city and her hometown until she was about 20 years old.

Her first single, 'Good Hurt', was released in the summer of 2017 and her first EP shortly after. The music sounds worlds away from the Chappell we know and love today. Far more grounded in indie and alternative palettes, her early catalogue feels right at home alongside the likes of London Grammar or Daughter – slow, emotional and raw with rich, velvety vocals. Even the artworks are painterly, ornate and in dramatic monochrome. Though she wrote from a similar place of bad decisions and emotional intimacy, it was more bleeding heart than payback time. During that time she went on to support Australian singer-songwriter Vance Joy on his tour, then British indie darling

Declan McKenna, before eventually moving to LA full time. It was that geographical shift that signalled a gear change for the young writer, both in terms of her personal life and her musical voice. Roan talks about it as a moment of coming into herself, with regards to her sexuality and her ability to live life fully as a queer woman. And of course, that poured out into the music she was making at the time, granting her permission to write songs as 'the real me', she once described.

After a few years of self-discovery, heartbreak and some new collaborators, we started to hear (and see) the early twinklings of Chappell's appeal today. Nostalgia-tinged synth-pop echoes and earworm hooks, campy sequin jumpsuits, roller skates and feather hats on the single artworks. What followed was yet more ups and downs, trials and promises, and eventually the perfect alignment of opportunities for fans to find and fall in love with her in ways no one could have predicted.

The allure has been undeniable; to see someone so rooted in the iconic sound of the past and yet bringing something entirely new to the pop music landscape, through a lens that is fresh, fun and completely unapologetic. Roan has breathed new life into a genre with pomp, spectacle and imagination. And she's done so while existing loudly in her own queer identity, uplifting the communities around her, championing the marginalised and asserting boundaries for herself and others. That's

DID YOU KNOW?

Chappell Roan's stage name is a tribute to her late grandfather. His name was Dennis K Chappell and his favourite song was 'The Strawberry Roan' by Curley Fletcher. She previously uploaded covers under the name 'Kayleigh Rose' but made the switch in 2016, the year he passed away.

There have been a lot of debates and confusion online as she's risen to fame about how to say her name. But really, the pronunciation is super simple. It's 'Chappell' like you'd pronounce the word 'chapel' and 'Roan' like you might say 'moan' or 'loan'. For example, 'Could you loan me your *The Rise and Fall of a Midwest Princess* vinyl indefinitely, it's a musical emergency.'

what makes this phenomenon all the more captivating to watch.

This book is a celebration of the extraordinary journey of an extraordinary artist and the movement that her success has ushered in. We'll explore all of the fascinating lore that has brought Chappell to where she is today and the lessons we can learn along the way, to thrive and flourish on our own extraordinary paths. Arming you with the inspiration, wisdoms and tips and tricks to be your absolute best self, to ride the peaks and troughs of life with belief, to find the fun, to love without fear and to embrace true, uncompromising authenticity, always.

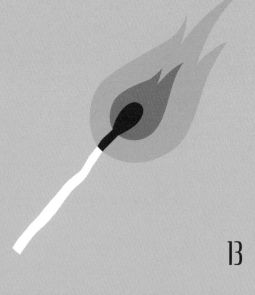

1

10 YEARS

IN THE

MAKING

'IT'S SO CLICHÉ, BUT IF YOU JUST DON'T STOP, YOU MAKE IT EVENTUALLY. FOR ME, I WAS SO MUCH CLOSER THAN I THOUGHT I WAS.'

It feels like Chappell Roan has had one of the swiftest ascents to global stardom of our generation, with her name and lyrics suddenly being uttered everywhere overnight.

But actually, her ascension was 10 years in the making. A decade of highs and lows, wins and failures, vision and precarity, all motored by the 26-year-old popstar's relentless grind and determination. When asked about the journey in her *Q* interview with Tom Power, she put it simply: 'It's so cliché, but if you just don't stop, you make it eventually. For me, I was so much closer than I thought I was.'

Born and raised in Willard, Missouri, to a deeply religious and culturally conservative family (we'll get more into her hometown later), baby Chappell wanted to flee. Entering singing competitions in her preteens and taking acting classes shortly after, music swiftly became an outlet for all her pent-up frustrations and emotions. Away at summer camp one year, she took her first foray into songwriting and came home with a handful of originals. Shortly after, encouraged by family and friends who had been supporting her singing for years, she did what all Gen Z/Millennial-cusp theatre kids did ... she started a YouTube channel. On it she posted what were then sultry, brooding, Tumblr kid-adjacent covers of songs she loved, as well as some of her own work, and she began to build up a small audience. In fact, popstar Troye Sivan – who was famous YouTuber Troye Sivan back then – even tweeted about one of her covers that he had listened to 'on repeat for 2 months,' he said.

17

'This has been in the making for a decade.'

It didn't take long for labels to start circling, and Chappell – going by Kayleigh Rose at the time – was off to New York for showcases. In 2015, at the age of just 17, she signed to Atlantic Records and the journey began. Back and forth between her hometown and Los Angeles between the ages of 18 and 20, before settling in California, Roan was determined to get her career off the ground. She released her debut EP *School Nights*, toured with Vance Joy and Declan McKenna, and met her now long-time collaborator Dan Nigro in 2018. She describes the time as 'a very intense experience', often through slightly gritted teeth. But at the same time as Chappell had been undergoing this chaos in her professional career, she'd also been navigating a personal liberation – relishing in the ability to live and explore the world as a queer woman for the first time since leaving Missouri. And while she was definitely making headway, unbeknownst to her, in walked Covid-19.

A victim of the music industry crash of the pandemic, Chappell's momentum was bucked before she had truly hit the runway. 'My relationship ended with my label like a lot of artists ended their relationships in 2020,' she told Tom Power with a shrug. 'You just get dropped if you're not making money in 2020.' When the world stopped with the pandemic, artists weren't able to tour – a primary source of income for so many, as well as a huge aspect of growth and marketing. Within the same week, she was also broken up with by her long-term boyfriend (yes, you read that correctly). The fall was swift and brutal.

'My relationship ended with my label like a lot of artists ended their relationships in 2020, you just get dropped if you're not making money in 2020.'

FUN FACT

When Chappell Roan signed her first major label deal at the age of 17, her school announced it over the intercom system. They shouted her out with a quick 'Congratulations, Kayleigh' before swiftly moving on to reel off what was on the menu for lunch that day!

'It feels like I was right all along.'

Now, I don't need to tell you where we're at today, but I will give you a whistle-stop tour of how we got here, from there, because it's a testament to patience and the long road. Discarded by Atlantic Records, Roan had no choice but to go it alone and follow her instincts. Towards the end of her label journey with Atlantic, she'd dabbled in a new creative and sonic direction. In fact, one of the last songs she released with them was a little single called 'Pink Pony Club', alongside 'Love Me Anyway' and 'California'. The tracks had done okay but they hadn't set the world alight, probably because the world had practically stopped spinning and Roan was already on the outs with her team.

Now at a critical life junction – one where you start rethinking every decision you've ever made, praying to whatever you believe in that one day you'll be able to look back at this moment and laugh – Chappell decided to lock in. She worked as a barista, a nanny and on productions to make ends meet, her music career steadily simmering in the background. Tidbits of press starting to bubble and conversation began to swirl, but it would take time before she could truly capitalise on it, with her main producer Nigro fully embroiled in the world of all things Olivia Rodrigo for her debut album. It was at this point, burnt and fatigued by the industry, that she started to truly question whether music was the path she was meant to be on. Roan ran out of money, moved back home to her parents' house and picked up a job at her local drive-thru. And so she made herself a promise. Give it one more shot, she vowed. One more year.

'It's finally paying off, all these interviews, all this travelling, all these failures of whatever, actually just led up to this.'

After some time recuperating back in the Midwestern plains, Chappell made the pilgrimage back to Los Angeles and the grind began again. After signing a Sony publishing deal, Roan soon reconnected with Nigro and the pair started working together again. She'd end up recording backing vocals for a number of Olivia Rodrigo's songs before eventually opening for her on the Sour Tour, all while releasing singles of her own, too, and converting fans bit by bit. The next year she went on her own tour, as the earliest iteration of the Chappell we see today, glammed to the gawds with drag queen openers. Her visual for 'Casual' was even a self-directed number of her atop a dirt bike. For Roan, 2023 was basically a year of laying the foundations

– more singles, her debut album release and a headline global tour, through to the top of 2024. While her work was definitely gaining her attention and fans, nobody could have predicted what would come next.

At the end of her tour, Roan went back on the road with her trusty friend Olivia Rodrigo as the tour opener for her sophomore album. Within just a week in front of these massive crowds, Roan's streams had seen a huge uptick. As soon as people saw and heard her, the impact was instant. The tour also coincided perfectly with her own promo in the form of a few key, viral live performances, including NPR's beloved Tiny Desk Concert. Chappell made sure to make an impression, wearing a red beehive wig adorned with cigarette butts, full drag princess glam and red lipstick deliberately smudged across her teeth, she had the crowd in the palm of her hands. She even stopped mid show to take some film pics and text on a bedazzled flip phone. Her razor-sharp vocals cut through the air and her melodrama drove home the sheer quality of her classic songwriting.

When the world finally woke up to her talent, or it hit the right audience, or she grew into who she was, it turned out to be a blessing that Chappell was free to carve her own path on her own terms. As the major-label wolves circled for the second time, Roan ended up signing with her producer Dan Nigro's label imprint Amusement in a collaboration that would benefit her ten-fold, under Island

Records. In her *The Face* cover interview, she laughed, 'I probably have one of the best deals ever in modern music because I was like: "F*ck you, guys, give me what I want or I'm going to do this myself."' By the time her follow-up single 'Good Luck, Babe!' dropped in April 2024, the world was already enthralled. And if ever a song was made to meet the challenge of expectations, it is this one. A biting falsetto anthem about being in love with someone who's in denial about who they are and the inevitable knowledge that it'll come back to bite them in the butt, the hyper-specific lyricism was no match for how compelling and all-consuming the track feels. The song explores how we can all relate to that kind of vicious hope to be able to tell those who have wronged us that special phrase: that we told them so. Add in the whimsical vocals of a modern Kate Bush and the cutting hook and you have yourself a certified hit on your hands.

It charted instantly across streaming sites and *Billboard*, Chappell's newfound audience from all the tour dates and viral clips, hungry and primed for new material. In fact, the song broke her success open so wide that it led even *more* people back to her album. When she played Coachella, her first ever festival slot, the tent was full to the brim – her set was the viral standout across both weekends. She was invited to the White House and happily declined. Her set at Lollapalooza had to be upgraded to the main stage. Almost a year after her album dropped, Chappell fever was at an all-time high and *The Rise and Fall of a Midwest Princess* hit number 1 in the *Billboard* Charts and number 1 in the UK Albums Chart. She has performed on *Saturday Night Live*, been nominated for six Grammys and took home Best New Artist at the 2024 Grammys and at the MTV VMAs, dedicating the latter trophy to the LGBTQIA+ community.

The best part is that Chappell's star shows no signs of falling. While we all catch up to where she already was over a year ago, she's been expanding and creating and honing her craft. Her winding journey seems to have been divinely timed and there's such a valuable lesson here in trusting your instincts faithfully if you want to find your people. She put it simply in an interview with Australian radio station Triple J: 'I just wrote a song that I loved and put it out. That is going to be the blueprint for everything else.' It's safe to say that the phenomenon of her rise brings a whole new meaning to the phrase, 'if you build it, they will come.'

'I probably have one of the best deals ever in modern music because I was like: "F**k you, guys, give me what I want or I'm going to do this myself."'

Girl Failure Watchlist

If you're looking for some inspiration of your own from imperfectly perfect femme heroines, who pick themselves up a thousand times over, trusting in the belief that it might all work out, look no further. Not every one of these stories has a neat or happy ending, but you know what? That's kind of the point. It's probably not the end.

FILMS

The Worst Person in the World (2021) directed by Joachim Trier

Frances Ha (2012) directed by Noah Baumbach

Shiva Baby (2020) directed by Emma Seligman

Sick of Myself (2022) directed by Kristoffer Borgli

The Miseducation of Cameron Post (2018) directed by Desiree Akhavan

The Edge of Seventeen (2016) directed by Kelly Fremon Craig

Obvious Child (2014) directed by Gillian Robespierre

Ghost World (2001) directed by Terry Zwigoff

Lady Bird (2017) directed by Greta Gerwig

Ingrid Goes West (2017) directed by Matt Spicer

Easy A (2010) directed by Will Gluck

Juno (2007) directed by Jason Reitman

Paris, 13th District (2021) directed by Jacques Audiard

Runaway Bride (1999) directed by Garry Marshall

Return to Seoul (2022) directed by Davy Chou

BOOKS

Happy Hour by Marlowe Granados

Conversations with Friends by Sally Rooney

Big Swiss by Jen Beagin

Such a Fun Age by Kiley Reid

I'm a Fan by Sheena Patel

Assembly by Natasha Brown

Rosewater by Liv Little

Cleopatra and Frankenstein by Coco Mellor

2

MIDWEST
PRINCESS

From her debut album title to her tour to her merch line, the phrase 'Midwest Princess' has become forever intertwined with Chappell Roan. In this chapter we're going to break down exactly what it takes to be a Midwest Princess, why Chappell is such a unique one and how you can embody its spirit, too. So aside from the camouflage shorts and pink Von Dutch she pulled together on her themed tour moodboards, what exactly does the term mean? Let me paint a picture for you, if I may.

Born in Willard, Missouri, to veterinarian mother Kara and nurse and practitioner father Dwight, Chappell came into the world as Kayleigh Rose Amstutz on 19 February 1998. When people invoke 'the Midwest' – states like Iowa, Nebraska, Kansas, Michigan or Minnesota – there's often a sense of quaintness and simple lives. The people are seen as fairly traditional and the salt of the earth. It's fair to say that the city of Willard doesn't stray too far from those ideals. Known at least in part for its agriculture and stone production, and with a population of less than 6,500, you can imagine a place that's equal parts industrial and lush with farmlands and natural landscapes. Rural is a word that might even spring to mind.

Born in a trailer park as the oldest of four children, when Chappell recalls her hometown, it's a place that's unsurprisingly a fairly religious and conservative community. From attending Christian summer camps to going to church as regularly as three times a week, it's a far cry from the glitz and glam of pink pony clubs and Hollywood boulevards. And yet it was at these very camps and in this town that she was able to sharpen her songwriting pen and flex her musicality as a preteen. In fact, the high school she attended has been nationally recognised for its music education. If she isn't a testament to that, I don't know what is.

'I have to honour this place that raised me. No matter how I feel about it, it's just always going to be a part of me.'

Though Chappell speaks about often sitting on her porch in the early hours of the morning, listening to Lana Del Rey and fantasising about escaping her small town life, with the choice to bring that heritage into her identity even at this stage, it's safe to say there's a side of Chappell that holds real love for aspects of her upbringing. In the Homecoming episode of her YouTube documentary *The Rise and Fall of a Midwest Princess*, she gushes about her love of nature, peace and catching frogs as she wades through a stream in platform Crocs, admitting it's harder to tap into those things back in LA, in the universe of her work. There's a sense of balance and grounding in that world that plays off the extroverted persona we've come to celebrate in her today. Throughout the entire series, the shots of the surrounding scenery look as if they were plucked straight from an old Windows screensaver. Google it if you're a little too young for that reference.

Even through her tour, Roan has spoken about making the conscious effort to visit and play in some of the smallest, most underserved corners of the country, presumably to go and reach those growing up just like she did. She was pleasantly surprised to see so many young queer people showing up in these spaces just to watch her perform. It's beautiful to think that a new generation of young LGBTQIA+ music fans now have these pockets of community to congregate and geek out within their Midwest contexts, in the very same place that she felt so isolated.

Ways To Bring A Little Peace Into Your Life

Forest Bathing

The Japanese practice of forest bathing is proven to have huge benefits on health and wellbeing when incorporated into modern lives. It sounds very grand but it can really be done in any green spaces you have available near you – your local park, the green at your school campus, that patch of grass in your shared garden, they all work too. It's all about taking a moment to find the calm and immerse yourself in the natural world around you. Whether it's 15 minutes or two hours, try switching your phone off, observing what you see, hear and smell around you. Consciously take note of your breathing, your pace if you're walking and keep your eyes open to take in the rich hues of nature, too.

Nature Sounds

If you live in a city where there's a general buzzing hum of traffic and yelling and bin trucks that your brain might not even register as noise anymore, tapping into nature sounds is an incredible way to soothe your nervous system, such as storm noises, ocean sounds, bird song or a full forest soundscape. Whether you're using them to help you fall asleep or focus while doing work, there are so many amazing free resources that you can play on loop to tap into your inner explorer and drown out the sonic clutter.

Be A Water Baby

I know it sounds basic but the healing qualities of being near a body of water cannot be understated. In our minds we feel like the local pond or muddy brown ripples of a nearby river are not really comparable to the crashing waves of the Indian Ocean, but in reality we have to take what we can get. And big or small, these pockets of nature enrich our souls. Gravitate towards water wherever you can, even if it's laps at the community pool on a Saturday morning, and I promise you will feel more grounded than ever. It's a great way to completely disconnect from the digital world of distractions while also relying on your own senses and moving your body in a meditative way.

Get Your Craft On

Who knew that Chappell was a crafter? Finding something creative to get stuck into can do wonders for your nervous system. Finding that 'flow state' where you are focused solely on the task in front of you – be it crocheting or sewing a new outfit, drawing, painting, or any other creative pursuit you feel like having a go at – can help your mind, body and breath to slow down and will help you find a bit of peace in our crazy, fast-paced society.

A lot of people don't realise I sew a lot, craft and crochet. I love throwing craft night at my house, like one or twice a week, and invite people over and make hot cocoa.

'There's a lot of value in the culture and fashion and music that a lot of the fashion world would maybe not deem as valuable.'

So how can I embrace my own Midwest Princess mentality, you ask? Well, the saying is that charity starts at home, and the same can be said of Midwest Princessing. We all have aspects of ourselves and our upbringing that we might feel don't quite match up with where we're at now or where we want to be. What we sometimes forget is just how valuable those parts of us truly are, both as an element of our story and as the dimensions that make us most unique.

Chappell proudly wearing the badge of Midwest Princess is about owning and loving the most non-conformative, aesthetically non-aesthetic parts of your story and making them your superpower. Reclaiming them and holding them up in a new light as something quirky and wonderful about you. Sometimes in the journey to get to where we're going, we feel like we have to leave everything behind, in the search for constant transformation and improvement. But we are allowed to be all of the contradicting things all at once, too. In fact, walking the tightrope of that balance is where all the most exciting things happen; to be soft and hard, glam and tacky, girly and rugged, small town and big city.

Think about what aspects set you apart from those around you now, and when you find them, love them the hardest. How might you be able to harness them, bring them into your present and use them for good? Can you be the representation of the place you grew up in that you never got to see? What would your younger self want to see in the world? What were they obsessed with and is there a way to reimagine it for yourself now?

3

PINK
PONY
CLUB

'Now, I am the girl who does the Britney routine; I am the girl who plays dress-up. I'm making up for that time. When I realised that I should dedicate my career to honouring the childhood I never got, it got big quick.'

Coming from a small town like Willard, Missouri, it's not hard to imagine that the paths laid out for someone like Chappell probably didn't include performing in arenas in full drag makeup and singing songs about lesbian love affairs to thousands of adoring fans. But ever since she was a teenager, something in her gut told her she was destined for something great – beyond what she could see around her.

Leaving the place you've always known for greener pastures is how the stories of so many greats start, from Dolly Parton to Joni Mitchell. But in reality, it's not all roses. It takes so much more courage, grit, determination and even failures than you might think. Even when things are going well you can feel a sense of guilt for leaving behind those you love or longing for the familiar and safe.

Chappell Roan's anthemic 'Pink Pony Club' tells the heart-wrenching tale of that exact kind of push and pull. When your worlds – past, present and future – collide and it feels like you have to make the ultimate choice. That just because you're gaining something beautiful, doesn't mean it comes without a cost. It's a song about finding the fire to persist and the courage to live in your truth, even when the people you hold dearest may not always get it.

Chappell wasn't always a performer. For a lot of her childhood, she was more of a problem child, dealing with a lot of frustration and depression and struggling in different ways to cope with it all. Even the visual for the track shows the journey to performance as one with a slow build and release in the end, a way to express herself boldly, shake loose from the baggage and forge forward with new community and freedom. For her, so much of that liberty came from finding a home in the queer communities of Los Angeles and falling in love with drag, a culture that still has a heavy influence in her aesthetics today, with drag performers often opening for her on tour too. It's an art form that's rooted in joyful defiance, where artists craft alter egos and perform in playful theatrics. Coming from a more conservative background, restricted by the rules and regulations of religion and tradition, the world of drag was a polar opposite to that of Chappell's childhood. She found a home in the irresistible sense of utopia and a world of endless possibilities where everyone can be anyone and anything can happen. And it was there that her truest self emerged – the self that loves hard, takes no prisoners and knows how to put on a damn good show.

'The project gives people an opportunity to express themselves without judgment and with freedom, to discover themselves in the same way that I feel like the project allows me to discover myself.'

Finding Your Own Pink Pony Club

At the heart of it, the concept of a Pink Pony Club is limitless, too. It's community, it's freedom, it's a sigh of relief. Your very own Pink Pony Club might look different to Chappell's, it's finding a place where you feel like you belong and allowing yourself to be found there too. It could take the form of joining a crafts club, picking up a new sport, learning a new instrument, maybe it's trying out a hobby you've always been too afraid to even think about, like stand up or singing. Ultimately, the message is that the firmer you stand in the things that bring you joy and make you who you are, the more likely you are to attract others who believe in and love the same things. Because how else can your people find you if you don't put yourself out there in the first place?

To get to that place, we have to take stock of how we feel around the people in our lives. Who do you feel the most calm around? Who do you not have to explain yourself to? Is there someone you feel comfortable sitting in total silence with? When was the last time you laughed until your stomach hurt, and who was it with? You know that moment when you leave a hangout with someone, who leaves you feeling exhausted and who leaves you feeling energised? Those are your people, pour into the bonds that feed you and bring you peace, and nurture them into your very own Pink Pony Club.

> *'This job allows me to do and be whoever I want, because there's no boundaries. And that was like the point of it all, to be anything I wanted.'*

And that's not to say that your identity is fixed forever, the beauty of relationships and perspectives is that they're ever-changing. In fact, a lot of the magic of Chappell lies in her unpredictable growth and constant transformation. She's vulnerable and takes no prisoners, she shows up in full glam on stage and fresh-faced in interviews. One day she's dressed as the Statue of Liberty, the next a Coke-bottle-shaped diva. Chappell even said of her career, during her self-produced documentary, 'This job allows me to do and be whoever I want, because there's no boundaries. And that was like the point of it all, to be anything I wanted.' She's all things all at once and you can be too.

Chappell has been morphing and transforming into her own wildest dreams, defying expectations and carving her own lane, and who knows where this journey might take her, or any of us for that matter. Once you've found that power within yourself to trust your own instincts and commit fully to self-expression, the possibilities of who you can become are endless. And as long as you let it guide and fuel you, you can't set a foot wrong.

4

HOW TO BE AUTHENTICALLY YOU

'I'VE NEVER NOT
BEEN MYSELF.
I'M REALLY GLAD
THE PERSONA
THAT I HAVE,
THE DRAG
VERSION,
IS STILL VERY
MUCH ME.'

Authenticity is a word that gets thrown around a lot these days. It's all well and good to dream of living your best life in theory, but it can be so much harder to action it in practice. We are people with lives and friends and families and jobs and dreams and responsibilities, after all, and our choices do come with real-life consequences. So how does one *actually* tap in and live as their most authentic self all the time? What if you don't even know who that person is?

Follow The Joy

The first step is simple. Focus on your strengths and the things that make you happiest in life. Often we think that we have to identify and hyperfixate on all of our flaws in order to better ourselves and grow as people. We're in an endless flux of self-improvement. Most of the time the opposite is true. You know that feeling when you're deep in a funk, maybe you're bedrotting on a Sunday morning and you'd planned to get up at 7am and go to that yoga class or clean your room, but the lie in was too enticing. You spiral into negative self-talk about how you're lazy and you failed and the day's already wasted. Next thing you know it's 3pm and you've wiled the hours away without moving an inch, and you didn't even have much fun while you were at it. Notice how when you swap that guilt and shame for acceptance, and rest in the hope that there will always be another chance to give it a go, it's way easier to forgive yourself and move past that small failure. You might have missed that class this morning, but there's still time to go and do that food shop or call your mum back. It feels counterintuitive, but when we feel most stagnant and lost, it's our smallest wins that build up energy, momentum, happy chemicals (whatever you want to call it) and eventually spur us into action. If your to-do list is 17 items long and it feels like you're never going to get anything done, start with the tiniest task first and work your way up.

The same is true for life's bigger questions. When you're trying to figure out what you want to do with your life or how to be a better version of yourself, don't start with all the things you're *not* doing well enough. Start with the things you *are* and the rest will follow. Yes, you might be a little disorganised, but when are the times when the motivation does strike you effortlessly? You may be terrible at self-promotion, but what's something that the person who knows you best would compliment you on? If you could be remembered for one thing in life, what would it be? Say you found out tomorrow that the concept of money was abolished and you never had to pay rent again, how would you want to spend your days? Finding a future that you truly love starts with growing those small seeds of positivity into your larger purpose. If you can figure out how to spend more time doing the things you're already good at, you'll find the hard stuff starts to feel a whole lot easier too.

Honesty Is The Best Policy

Being #positive doesn't mean we want to live in La La Land either. The very definition of authenticity is the act of being genuine and real – two traits that require honesty. Once you understand more about yourself and accumulate a healthy list of the things you love about yourself, it's also important to make sure you're telling the truth, both to yourself and to those around you.

And no, that doesn't mean being unkind or rude or 'telling it how it is', like they always seem to say on reality TV shows. Being honest doesn't mean being without care. In fact, when it comes to being honest with those close to you, it's an act of deep care and love. If a friend hurts you and it goes unaddressed, that small wound can fester and create deeper cracks between you. In that sense open communication is not just a pledge to be true to yourself, but also an investment in the relationships that you cherish, to make sure that they last as long as possible and are as healthy as they can be.

That same truth-telling has to extend inwards, too. While we don't champion negative self-talk in this house, we definitely do advocate for transparency, especially of the emotional variety. We can all fall victim to storytelling when it comes to ourselves or getting swept up in narratives that don't serve us. Whether it's saying that we're fine when we're not, telling ourselves there are things we can't do without ever trying them or straight up just ignoring and abandoning our desires and needs. Authenticity requires regular emotional reality checks. Does this still feel good to me? Am I sure this is what I need? Am I doing this for the right reasons? Whether it's journalling, sending voice notes, making video diaries or taking long, pensive bus rides, make sure you're making time to check in with yourself as often as you can, as you would with any good friend.

'My career has worked because I've done it my way, and I've not compromised morals and time. I have not succumbed to the pressure.'

Face Your Biggest Fear

The very nature of authenticity is that you are allowing your truest self to be seen. One of the most intimidating parts of that fact is that it comes with a money-back guarantee that you will not be for everyone. The idea of that alone is daunting, because if and when that rejection comes it can feel so deeply personal. But don't worry, that's only because it is! You are being you, and there is not a single 'you' in the world that is u...niversally appealing. It would be a very boring world if there was.

Chappell is an incredible example of this. With the hypervisibility that has been thrust on her in the last couple of years and for all the praise showered on her, there has also been an inevitable wave of critique. People who don't like her tone or think she's ungrateful or overrated or maybe they just don't get it.

We have to practise resting easy in the knowledge that if someone doesn't like you when you're being yourself, that's fine. Because you still get to be who you are. They were never meant for you anyway. In the worst possible alternative timeline where you aren't staying true to yourself, you end up changing and shifting and moulding for other people's approval, imagine it's people-pleasing 7.0. Now I'll let you in on a secret. Even in that universe, there will *still* be people who aren't fans, because that's just how it works. So if you're damned if you do and damned if you don't, why wouldn't you at least pick the timeline where you honour yourself?

'I'd be more successful if I wore a muzzle.'

Internal Vs External

A lot of our anxieties around who we are and who we want to be can be boiled down to two schools of thought: factors that are internally motivated and ones that are externally motivated. Your internal motivations are self-generated: self-esteem, emotions, thoughts, morals, beliefs about the world, for example. Your external motivations come from outside of yourself: factors like the views of others, social media, critical acclaim, money, prestige.

Now, one is not necessarily better than the other – most people fall somewhere on a spectrum of finding one kind more compelling than the other. But wherever your tendencies lie, it's a super-useful metric for investigating our desires and goals in life, the places that we seek validation from and making sure we're covered across all bases as a failsafe. Sometimes considering external factors can be extremely valuable in excelling at something we love. Shouting about your work on social media can be a great way to reach new audiences, communicate your experience and attract more work back to you. Certain opportunities or institutions might be a great addition to a CV even if they aren't your ultimate end goal. On the reverse, some of that external validation can feel fleeting or out of your control. That's why it's important to make sure you also have sources that you can generate internally to feel fulfilled and secure in yourself and the things you do. When artists like Chappell speak about writing songs for themselves or feeding their inner child, it speaks to that same infinite resource. Do something for the pure, innate love of it. It's come from within you and so it's always guaranteed. That's what will sustain you in the moments where everything else is on shaky ground.

'I had to let go of the adult in me that thought, "oh, I need to be so sophisticated and serious and so good at everything or else I'm not good enough."'

Bring People In

As Chappell has shown time and time again, there's no better way to rise than with a community around you. While you shouldn't need them to validate your existence, you certainly can lean on them for support and companionship when times do get tough (and also when they're good!).

Being authentic doesn't mean you don't get to ask for help, it actually means the opposite. The more in tune you are with yourself, the more you'll learn to practise discernment. And the more you'll attract people who are drawn to you wholeheartedly. That's how the most beautiful communities are formed! When you're in a place where you feel safe, comfortable and seen by those around you, bring people along on the journey with you. Tell them what your goals and dreams are, ask them to hold you accountable, show them your vulnerabilities and find encouragement in them on those days when you do have doubts.

5

LOVER
GWORL

From 'Casual' to 'Good Luck, Babe!' so much of Chappell's art deals with the wonderfully raw realities of loving out loud. Sometimes your heart chooses the wrong person by accident and you're left to pick up the pieces, other times you might make bad romantic choices just because you can or because you have faith that it may all turn out okay. While navigating the world with that kind of heart-on-sleeve abandon leaves you open to an entire minefield of hurt and heartbreak, it's also one of the bravest things a person can do in this day and age. Not to be 'we live in a society' but ...

We actually do live in a society where it feels terrifying to put yourself out there. In a time post-pandemic where the streets are filled with grass-is-always-greener philosophers, serial ghosters, dating-app addicts and viral seekers recording strangers and putting them on the internet, vulnerability is getting scarcer and scarcer. We are losing the art of connecting with others and we also don't know who we can trust. Being open about your feelings and intentions has never felt riskier.

'It's my favourite part of life, having a crush on someone. It's the best thing ever when you are at the beginning of a relationship and talking on FaceTime for eight hours a day.'

And if you do leave yourself open to love and find yourself heartbroken, it can feel even more daunting to be open and honest about that. Whether that's to ask for help or simply to share what you've been going through. It's all well and good to preach self-love and learn to find beauty in your own company, but companionship with others is also a natural human desire. Romance doesn't have to become obsolete just because we love ourselves too. How are we supposed to find it if we're shamed for admitting we want it in the first place?

The ups and downs of keeping her heart and her hurt wide open for the world to see and feel is part of what makes Chappell's music so relatable and all-consuming. In an interview with *Rolling Stone*, Roan unpacked details about the relationship that inspired much of her modern heartbreak hit 'Casual'. After a long-distance romantic connection was sparked with someone online where they were emotionally vulnerable and intensely connected, from her perspective at least, the pair met and Chappell was hooked. But only a week later, the person broke the news that they'd met someone else. Not long after, Chappell also discovered that the person had downplayed their connection to mutual friends as something casual, while telling her the opposite thing. The musical result was a song filled with frustrations and lost hopes about the confusing disconnect that often crops up between people's actions and their words in the modern dating landscape.

It's like we crave closeness and intimacy on a level deeper than our conscious minds are willing to admit, reaching out to each other and voicing feelings without always thinking about the consequences of that. Or we're on the other side of the equation, open and willing, but trying to navigate the possibilities of scaring someone off or showing our hand too soon and giving them all the power.

FUN FACT

Have you ever heard of 'limerence'? If you're chronically online, chances are you're already familiar with this, but if not, allow me to ruin your day a little. Limerence is basically a term for that intense feeling of longing or obsession that you develop when you're caught in the tenterhooks of a bad crush. You know when you zone out for 10 minutes while your friend is talking because you can't stop imagining a future together or you rush to bed early just so you can maximise the time you have to fantasise about possible scenarios you might find yourself in with them. When you hover over their Instagram page with featherlight precision so that you can scroll all the way back to their first post in 2016 and work your way back up to the top. Or you have to mute their stories because you watch them so quickly and linger so long that the app starts serving you them the very minute they post. The sickness of it all!

Well, it turns out that quite often that feeling is less about the person you're fantasising over and more about the idea of them or the addictive flutter of romance itself. For me, the concept definitely doesn't drain the fun out of having crushes itself, but it is a useful tool to dig into if you ever find yourself at the point where the butterflies you're feeling over someone start to sour into real anxiety or intrusive thoughts about yourself. Sometimes your brain is overridden with chemicals and it can be important to ground yourself in the knowledge that you are just a person and so are they. It's important not to get too carried away with the fictionalised idea or thing they represent to you. With or without them, you will be fine. And you never know, maybe they chew too loud or sleep with their eyes open or something and you just haven't had time to fill in the blanks yet.

Bring Back Yearning

So, sleep icks aside, how do we bring back real lovers? It's clear that so many of us, even those of us who weren't alive back when you could meet the love of your life at your local coffee shop, are desperate to return to a world of romantic possibilities and fleeting flirty encounters. Here's a guide to ways to put yourself out there and leave yourself open to potential connections in the real world.

Be Adventurous

When looking for love, it's crucial to be open-minded and expand your routines. To be clear, I do not mean be reckless. Safety is key, especially with dating. Be adventurous in your day-to-day life by attending new events you don't usually go to, trying out that new café around the corner that's selling matcha lattes, stroll around the farmers' market in a new neighbourhood. You will only find the same results if you continue to look in the same places. It's a great way to ensure that not only are you encountering new crops of people but you're also gaining from the experience either way, whether anything happens romantically or not. You never know what new passions or habits you might fall in love with along the way.

Be Curious

The girls are pretty good at this anyway, but curiosity really does fast-track connection. When you're speaking to someone new or see someone you like the look of, the most natural way to reach out is to ask them questions. If they talk about something they love, ask them why they love it. If they're wearing a nice shirt, ask them where they got it. That cute barista who just made your matcha latte at the new coffee shop round the corner, ask them what their name is. It's such an easy way to show willing and grease the wheels of conversation where so many of us are used to keeping it short and sweet. It also hopefully encourages them to find out more about you in return, even if they're just mirroring the behaviour.

Speak Your Truth

Okay, here comes the scary bit, but this is probably the most important one. Tell. The. Truth. If you ever come across dating experts on the internet, it's a truly depressing state of affairs. You'll hear them telling women to master all kinds of tools of coded language and restraint with the primary goal of not scaring away a potential partner. Newsflash: we should be trying to scare away the people that are fundamentally wrong for us! The most crucial thing you can do as a lover gworl looking to find your lover partner is to be honest about exactly where you're at and what you want. Give them and yourself an opportunity to assess and either choose to dip or move forward accordingly, with all the relevant information. I'll even take it a step further and say that we need to normalise being more upfront and honest with *everyone* around us about where we're at and what we want. We used to live in a world where friends would fix up other friends at dinner parties. Now we're lying to our besties, telling them we've cut off toxic talking stages, that we're still DMing or holding onto secret crushes on our mutuals who might be secretly just as into us too. Someone has to make the first move, stake their claim and be brave. It might as well be you.

No Such Thing As Romantic Failure

Last but not least, I want to remind you of the beautiful, freeing fact that actually every win is a win in the world of love. Human connection is a marvel and it's a strange myth we've created as a species that it can only be considered successful if it lasts forever. It's a mini miracle every time you cross paths with another human being who's able to make you really *feel* something and be a little more excited about the world. Relish every small moment of giddiness or anticipation as proof that you are alive and present and full of hope and love. See the people you meet as equals but not messiahs who can ordain you with a sense of worthiness and personhood. You were lovable before you met them and you will be lovable whether they stay or go. Lean in to the flirty fun of life, especially if you are single, and cherish the moments of true independence and endless possibilities and opportunities for entertaining new lore.

Real Lovers Watchlist

BUT I'M A CHEERLEADER (1999)
This satire features the great Natasha Lyonne, who's sent to a conversion camp when her parents begin to suspect she is 'a homosexual'. Also starring RuPaul and a host of other huge names, what ensues is a hilarious and tender journey of denial, rebellion and self-discovery.

PAST LIVES (2023)
For the true yearners out there. This film is not strictly a romance but is buzzing with what-ifs and unspoken moments. Exploring the Korean concept of in-yun (a belief that interactions in our lives are connected to events in our past lives) and the layers of fate that bring us to be the people we are today, both individually and in relation to each other.

CALL ME BY YOUR NAME (2017)
Timothée Chalamet altered everyone's brain chemistry with his performance as love-drunk Elio in this balmy 80s summer love story. Adapted from the novel by André Aciman and set in northern Italy, with a heart-wrenching Sufjan Stevens soundtrack, this film is guaranteed feels from beginning to end.

***ENTERGALACTIC* (2022)**
Created by Kid Cudi, this animated film is an intoxicatingly hazy story about sparks flying between two neighbours. From the soundtrack to the colour palette, the world it creates feels magnetic and warm – exactly how you might feel when sparks are flying.

***MOONLIGHT* (2016)**
This brooding queer masterpiece brings entirely new dimensions to definitions of identity, masculinity and sexuality with the context of African American men. It's about coming of age and coming into oneself, as well as the resilience of love and connection in even the most challenging of environments.

***MASTER OF NONE* (2015)**
This series is not just immaculately made but it also feels like a charmingly real and honest portrayal of what it's like to love in the modern age. From Aziz's own relationship toils to season three's focus on Denise's marriage, it finds the beauty in the failures and the richness in the mundane.

BOTTOMS (2023)

At first glance this film doesn't feel that romantic but when you think about it, is there anything more lover-girl-coded than starting a feminist fight club for the sole purpose of being able to spend time with your high school crush? *Bottoms* feels like the cinematic equivalent of Chappell's music – it's fun, it's flirty, it's a little ludicrous, it believes in love and it's unmistakably queer.

LOVE LIFE (2020)

This anthology series is seriously slept on. With the first season focusing on the romantic pursuits of Darby, played by Anna Kendrick, and the second on Marcus, played by William Jackson Harper, this show tracks their entire relationship timeline in snapshots. It's funny, it's sad, it's frustrating, it's sweet, it's exactly like dating in real life.

ETERNAL SUNSHINE OF THE SPOTLESS MIND (2004)

This classic is both soul-destroying and faith-restoring all at once. Starring Jim Carrey and Kate Winslet, it straddles the line between science-fiction and romantic drama. Centring around an unlikely couple stuck in the dilemma of a lifetime – deeply in love but potentially bad for each other. Investigating if love truly can conquer all and what role we have to play in resisting the fate in front of us.

BEFORE SUNRISE (1995)

This film is how every lover gworl daydreams that their summer of interrailing around Europe will go. Giddy and hopeful as two young people meet on a train in Vienna and spend the next day together exploring the city and getting to know each other. The first part in a trilogy that follows the same characters as they connect at different points in their lives.

ABOUT TIME (2013)

Tissues at the ready for this whimsical yet deeply grounded tale of love, loss and time travel. Asking questions like how far would you go to be with the people you love most and if you had the power to spend your time exactly as you pleased, how would you? It's a quaintly British generational epic that will leave you feeling so hopeful, present and grateful for your lot in life, whatever it is.

6

CAMP ROAN! HER STYLE EVOLUTION

While Chappell Roan has carved a lane for herself with her singular sonics, her commitment to visual extravagance has played just as big a role in her modern icon status. At every turn, she's found ways to be both daring and playful with her fashion and glam, leaning into the campy theatrics of drag queens and pop stars past with her own unique perspective. At her NPR Tiny Desk Concert, she wore a massive beehive wig adorned with a pink fluffy fan and tiara, a full marionette drag and deliberate lipstick smudged throughout her teeth. Her whole band matched her makeup style with streams of mascara and 80s-pop pink prom dresses. On tour, she has dressed up as everyone from Joan of Arc to the Statue of Liberty. So it's safe to say that she's not afraid to have fun with it. In this chapter we're going to dig into standout moments so far, exactly what makes her style so exciting and why silliness is something we should all bring into more of our everyday antics.

Glitz & Glam-Er

When it comes to her glam, and the hefty job it has to do in matching the energy of her trailblazing fits, Chappell has figured out the perfect balance of experimentation and trademark. Always equipped with a bright porcelain skin, theatrical eyes and bold, unexpected pops of colour, her editorial beauty looks add endless drama to an already pretty dramatic stage presence. Within those barriers that make her instantly recognisable – separating Chappell from

Kayleigh – her palette feels inspired in equal parts by so many cultural touchpoints.

Parts of it feel almost renaissance in the soft, blurry baby blues of her eye shadows and cherubesque rosy cheeks. Her flouncing auburn curls and baby fringe often hark back to flashy 80s retro aesthetics and the permed likes of Cyndi Lauper and Madonna. The exaggerated nature of the application is undoubtedly a tribute to the costumed stylings of all drag queens worth their salt. And there's an absurd regality to it that feels reminiscent of characters like Helena Bonham Carter's Queen of Hearts in *Alice's Adventures in Wonderland*. It's all tied together with an irreverence and disregard for the prescribed ideals of feminine beauty, something that restricts us mostly to rules set by the male gaze, mind you. And for all the historical references, that part feels utterly innovative and modern. Despite all the rich nods and influences, it's rare, if ever, that Chappell looks like anything we've ever seen before.

'I love looking pretty and scary, or pretty and tacky, or just not pretty, I love that too.'

In an interview with *Dazed* about how her glam has taken the beauty landscape by storm, one of her makeup artists, Sterling Tull, shares this wisdom that honestly speaks to a lot more than makeup: 'Do something that scares you. And if it doesn't work, it doesn't work. I hate seeing people discourage themselves. As long as you're putting makeup on your face, you're doing the damn thing. You can have lipstick on your teeth and it doesn't matter, as long as you have fun.' There's this sense in everything that Chappell does visually that feels like walking on a tightrope of risk, but that's where the most thrilling ideas occur. And it's far more exciting for everyone involved to dance on that shaky ground than to find your feet firmly planted in the mundane. We could all afford to be a little less concerned with being pleasing to the eye and a bit more empowered to be interesting. Whether your origin story is in gay clubs in LA or an underground art scene or the lush, verdant countryside. I'm setting you the challenge, the next time you're playing around with palettes before a shower, to try to tell that story through a makeup look. Don't be afraid of colour or shape and see what you can express purely for fun.

'I am not trying to be a chic b*tch. I love the chic b*tches, but I am not trying to be like that.'

Cool AF Makeup Accounts To Follow

Andrew Dahling (@1800andrewdahling)
Who better to start with than the person responsible for so many of Chappell's own best looks? Andrew's work is weird, wild and wonderful, often diving into the abstract and challenging the boundaries between beauty and straight-up art.

Raisa Flowers (@raisaflowers)
From Kelela to Saweetie, Raisa brings a dramatic drag flair to all of her artistic creations. Whether it's razor-sharp brows or neon colour pops, this NYC native prioritises authenticity and challenging conventions when it comes to her looks.

Isamaya Ffrench (@isamayaffrench)
Beauty without restraint is the line Isamaya lives by in her work. Beginning painting children's faces at parties to MUA gigs and editorial work, now with that ethos guiding her own renegade beauty brand ISAMAYA, her Instagram is the place to be if you want a glimpse into the cutting edge of beauty.

Leana Ardeleanu (@leana.ardeleanu)
Berlin-based MUA Leana has painted the faces of everyone from Noah Cyrus to Gabbriette. Her runway-ready briefs usually sit somewhere between gothic and fantasy, with an ultra-modern sheen, and are always provocative.

Naezrah (@naezrahlooks)
It's never a boring day on the feed of NYC-based artist and creative Naezrah. Her shapes are unorthodox and her palette is kaleidoscopic. Vocal and transparent about the battle she's faced as a dark-skinned woman in the beauty industry, her deeply original work has gained her hundreds of thousands of followers as well as a DM from SZA.

'I really love the Midwest and the fashion of gas stations and … I was born in a trailer park and I think that whole aesthetic, you can't really get it if you're not from there.'

Unlikely Fashionistas

When it comes to fashion, Chappell does not shy away from dirty words like 'tacky' or 'trashy'. In fact, she runs towards them. Whether it's harking back to her Midwestern roots and jewellery hauls from Claire's accessories to the fake-it-til-you-make-it costume culture of drag-queen aesthetics, or assless, studded leather chaps equipped with matching choker, Roan finds the editorial beauty in places that a lot of the mainstream don't bother to look. Chatting to Jimmy Fallon in her full ice queen *Swan Lake*-inspired get up, she explained how she works with her stylist, Genesis Webb, to pull from a vast range of places.

'My stylist Genesis Webb and I, we pull from drag, we pull from horror movies, we pull from burlesque, we pull from theatre.'

A fellow Midwestern Princess, Webb's own trajectory since teenagehood went from Tumblr famous to thrift reseller to jewellery brand owner, before eventually stumbling into styling during Covid when money was tight and she needed a pivot. She crossed paths with Chappell while assisting and the connection came fast and thick. The rest is quite literally history. Webb explained in a piece for

British *Vogue* how the pair's tastes complement to create the perfect alchemy: she taught me just that glam and colour and glitter can be just as avant-garde and just as high-fashion as anything.' Those two equal and opposite forces form that basis of Chappell's captivating style evolution, the soft and hard, the punk and pop, the regal and the trailer park. It's Vivienne Westwood and bright-pink prom dresses and a wig adorned with butterflies and cigarette butts.

Unserious Candidates

Now not everybody is going to be able to pull big-name designers or hire a creative director to help realise their sartorial visions. But at the heart of Chappell's aesthetic is something far more simple ... and free. And that is a true commitment to taking none of it too seriously. If all you can take away from her approach to glam is that it's exhilarating to live in a spirit of fun, then that is more than enough. Yes, it takes consideration and planning and bravery to step into unchartered territory and leave yourself open to ridicule and critique. But it also requires that you stop *caring* so much. Otherwise the anxiety would stop you in your tracks.

That much is also clear from Chappell's stage presence and the pure, ecstatic fun she encourages and embodies through her live show. From money guns to glitter balls, fundamentally, the world of Chappell Roan and her music is a neverending party. Sure, it's a party that takes you on an emotional rollercoaster – maybe at points you're crying outside in the smoking area or in a DMC with a long-lost friend, but at other times you're frolicking around in the living room or unapologetically hogging the aux cable. And the lesson we can all learn from *The Rise and Fall of a Midwestern Princess* is that life is not only more fun when you lean into the chaos, it's also a lot more beautiful.

In her interview with *Capital Buzz*, Chappell talks about the moment she realised she was allowed to have fun with her music. 'The idea sparked the first time whenever I went to the gay club for the first time. Because I was like "why am I so serious? Everyone here is having *so* much fun."' What followed was an intentional effort to create more music that wasn't only concerned with emotional release in the writing process, but that could also serve as a joyous emotional release through the act of performing it live over and over again. The Chappell we fell in love with is a Chappell who made music with the goal of having fun with it, songs that you wouldn't get bored of or depressed by. I think there's a sermon in there somewhere for those of us who waste time worrying about what others may think or expect of us, instead of doing what makes us happiest.

'I think what really made me feel like I could make "silly art" was once I got into therapy with inner child work and working on what did little me want.'

What's On The Dopamine Menu?

In theory we all know not to take life too seriously, but it can be harder to do in practice. We so easily find ourselves caught up in the grind and pressures of the day-to-day, navigating errands and tasks with the stress levels of an animal being hunted for sport, as they say. Dopamine menus can be a great way to yank yourself out of those cycles and get the happy chemicals flowing again.

It sounds more elaborate than the reality, but ultimately a dopamine menu is just a list of activities you have on deck that are guaranteed ways to boost your dopamine with minimal thought or exertion. We want that sweet, sweet rush to feel as painless as possible. It's a great way to practise mini-moments of mindfulness throughout your day, as well as encouraging better motivation, focus, emotional regulation and habit forming, too.

Here are some examples of items you might include on your own dopamine menu:

- *A bubble bath*
- *15-minute solo bedroom dance party*
- *A sweet treat from that expensive café around the corner*

- *Trying out a new recipe*
- *Watching an episode of your comfort show*
- *Practising deep breathing or guided meditation*
- *Taking a nap*
- *Treating yourself to a face mask*
- *Learning a few phrases in a new language*
- *Call or text a friend to check in*
- *Watching a vlog you like*
- *A cup of tea and your favourite snack*
- *Playing a boardgame with your roommates*
- *Listening to your favourite album or podcast*

The key to an effective menu is that it feels entirely bespoke to you and your interests and is also well-balanced. You can even go a step further to organise your menu like you would if you were actually constructing a meal. Splitting the activities into starters, mains, sides and desserts based on how big or small the dopamine hit might be. Your starters and sides may be more of the quick fixes, while your long-term goals constitute a main and anything that feels like an indulgence or self-care moment is a perfect dessert option. We need all of these different levels to feel truly energised and rejuvenated, but just like a real meal, we need each in moderation.

7

LET'S TALK ABOUT
BOUNDARIES

'I'm very turned off by the celebrity of it all. Some girls have been in this so long that they're used to that, but I'm not that girl.'

For all of the acclaim that Chappell has been showered with over the last year or so, it hasn't come without its complications. Now that her name is firmly planted in the public consciousness, it takes very little for her actions to spark lively debate. So when she took to TikTok to speak out about creepy fan behaviour, it wasn't long before the discourse spread like wildfire. In the video she directly expresses that just because she's famous now doesn't mean she actually enjoys fame or the expectations that come with it, namely people in the streets feeling entitled to her time, attention, hugs and friendship. 'I don't care that it's normal,' she said.

Now to some of us, that is not a controversial statement. When we see a famous person out in the world, we leave them be. At best, we might nod or apologise profusely before asking for a quick pic. But for many others, this move apparently felt like a slap in the face. The news went viral, with many dubbing Roan ungrateful and entitled, claiming she should just be happy for her success and swallow any shortcomings that come as part of that package deal. But in an age of ever-weirder behaviour and eroded social norms, it's not at all surprising that we're seeing so much dialogue about the perils of fame, fandom and celebrity culture. In an age of social media, conspiracy theories and invasive internet content, the relationship between artists and fans is more fraught than ever.

At the end of the day, if something makes you feel uncomfortable, no matter how lucky or otherwise happy you might be, you should absolutely feel entitled to voice that. And just because most fans are the reason for your success does not mean that a small minority of overstepping fans have a right to invade your personal space or privacy. In fact, it's pretty clear that the behaviour of the exceptions, in this case, are likely to be ruining it for those of us who follow the rules. And the more that we encroach on the private lives of those in the public sphere, the less capacity these artists will have to continue to share and create from. Like, do we want album two or not?!

'Everything that I really love to do now comes with baggage. If I want to go thrifting, I have to book security and prepare myself that this is not going to be normal. Going to the park, Pilates, yoga – how do I do this in a safe way where I'm not going to be stalked or harassed?'

Parasocial Activity

It's like we expect that anyone who ever has the fortune of living out their dream as an artist forfeits any and all rights to ever experience negative emotions ever again. Just because a fan base has uplifted you to where you are today, does not mean that you owe them all your basic privacy and respect.

The problem stems from the concept of fame itself, from the fascination with every minute detail of people's lives to this stubborn disconnect from the fact that they are just ... people. As much fun as it is to explore and dissect the brilliance of new budding stars that provide such rich material and inspiration to feed the next generation of young people and creative minds, that should not automatically translate to celebrity worship. We can be interested without being, well, weird about it.

It's an issue that has played out in different ways for generations, from paparazzi to tabloid culture and now weaponised internet armies and stalker behaviour. Tyler the Creator's single 'Noid' last year explored a similar topic of the paranoia that comes with being a modern-day public figure and I'd be lying if I didn't say the issue is made even more complicated by dynamics of race and gender too. For a lot of female pop stars, the expectations placed on them and how much of their lives must become public domain are totally unsustainable. It's a pattern that has harmed many a career already and shows no signs of stopping. We want constant access on social media, the

music has to be soul-bearing and diaristic and you have to break down every lyric and metaphor for us too, once it's out. We want to know who you're dating and who you got dumped by, where you got that top from, who did your makeup and also what you had for breakfast maybe. And after all of that is poured out, in your downtime in real life, when you're not Chappell, but trying to piece together what's left of your regular life as Kayleigh, how *dare* you want space from us to do your grocery shopping or check in to your flight in peace?

There's this tendency to resent when famous people complain about the trappings of fame, because of course they still do so from a place of immense privilege. But when you think about it, shouldn't we want more people in the limelight whose main goal is not to be worshipped by us? People who are fuelled by the art and the craft of it all, rather than how much money they can make or how many followers they have? It's like what the Greek philosopher Plato said about the best leaders being the people who do not seek power. I'd rather the reluctant star any day, wouldn't you?

What was so inspiring about this moment was that even with the dogpiling, Chappell didn't back down. Because ultimately, she's the only person who has to live her life, and all she can do is advocate for her own needs and boundaries, whether that makes the internet people angry or not. Those who are open to the feedback will move accordingly and those who are not, were never going to listen anyway.

How To Set Boundaries

Okay, so you may not be an internationally-acclaimed pop superstar but you may have your own gripes with how aspects of your life are going. Maybe your friends don't always make you feel included, or your parents invade your privacy, or your partner doesn't communicate well in moments of conflict. So here are a few tips and tricks that might be helpful if you ever feel like your boundaries are being crossed and you want to communicate that clearly, safely and respectfully.

Know What You Want

The first step in setting boundaries sounds obvious, but it's knowing what you want. Often when we're in a situation that we don't love, it's clear to us immediately. Maybe it feels bad in our body or we notice that we're more anxious or upset. Those cues are hard to miss. But what can be harder to pinpoint is what a better solution would be. Because knowing what we don't want is not always the same as knowing what we do. And with clear desires on our part, it can be really difficult to present and assert clear boundaries to those around us. Take time with yourself to ask what exactly about this is making me uncomfortable and why? What would I prefer instead? What could the person I'm communicating with do to help me reach that place of safety and security? How could we work together towards that?

I Vs. You

When talking about your feelings, try to stick to the use of 'I' rather than 'you', for example, 'It makes me feel like ...' or 'I am not comfortable when ...'. It removes some of the accusation and blame from the statement and brings it back to the impact it's having on you, something that it's far harder for the other person to seek to argue with or discredit. It also removes some of the risk of them becoming defensive, hopefully.

Consistency Is Key

A key when it comes to boundaries and the upholding of them in the long term is consistency. Communicating them in the first place can feel incredibly daunting, but actually, this might be the hardest step of all. Our brains assume that once the conversation has been had, that's it, job done. But actually boundaries are formed and solidified by your ability to stand on business as and when they are tested and crossed. Say, for example, someone tries to make you the butt of the joke when you're hanging out in a group setting and after weeks of discomfort you pull them aside to express that it makes you uncomfortable when they do that and ask them to stop. Maybe in that one-to-one conversation they apologise profusely for their behaviour, saying that they had no idea they were doing that. You leave the interaction feeling relieved and really heard. Things go well for a while but the next time you and your friends are all out at a party, they end up doing it again. That is the actual critical moment in the timeline, because now that you have covered all of your bases and voiced your boundaries, it's also up to you to stand firm in them. Whether that looks like calmly calling out the behaviour in that moment, removing yourself from the situation or reassessing whether the relationship is still tenable. Whatever feels most appropriate, it's just important that you demonstrate that a crossed boundary comes with consequences and that your word holds value at least to yourself. Because if you don't communicate that, you're subconsciously co-signing the opposite.

Make It Mutual

And the last step to mastering the art of boundary-setting is to be as good at respecting others as you are at asserting your own. Boundaries are a two-way street, they thrive when they are mutual and reciprocated. That's why the best way to encourage respect and care in the relationships you value is to model that behaviour yourself. When others express their needs and wants, make sure you listen and process, be generous with your apologies where necessary, remove shame from the equation and if you have to take time before responding to curb that fight or flight response, ask for that too.

And remember, if somebody's response to you asserting an important boundary is for them to flare up or refuse, that does not mean that you were wrong to express what you need in the first place. It means you might have just been asking the wrong person.

8

A PHENOMENON OF THE FEMME VARIETY

'WE'RE ALL SO DOWN TO BE BOLD.'

Don't you just love women? Chappell's track 'Femininomenon' explores that exact feeling. A slumber party banger about the magical ease of her relationships with women in almost direct contrast to what she'd experienced previously with men. Her discovery of her own sexuality as its own phenomenon to her – one of the feminine kind.

Expanding that even further, you can pretty much apply the same idea to Chappell's journey too. She's a queer pop phenomenon at a time and in a space where very few have made it before. And at the heart of everything she does is this bold embrace of femininity and power in both herself and others. From the way that she expresses her creativity visually to how she writes about sapphic romance to empowering women around her as part of her team. Even how she pays tribute to pop icons and historical figures of the past carries a feminist sheen. From dressing up as Joan of Arc in head-to-toe chainmail to a full teal Statue of Liberty costume, complete with assless chaps and comically large apple for her Governor's Ball performance. At Coachella she recreated the butterfly look of artist, activist and style icon Lady Miss Kier and she's also cited British fashion designer Vivienne Westwood as a huge source of inspiration. When it comes to her all-femme band and the bond they share on stage, the girls are a tight-knit group of instrumentalists who get just as stuck into the pageantry of Chappell's live shows as she does.

Spiritually, Chappell is a pop girly through and through, growing up in the golden era of MTV. She always takes a second to shout out the formative women who shaped her love of the genre, in an age where begrudging or pretending not to love fun music has become the norm. From raving about Katy Perry's 'Teenage Dream' and the impact it had on her, to channelling her inner Britney with extravagant live performances or crediting Rihanna's 'Stay' as one of the reasons she started writing music. Even as she's reached new heights of fame, Roan is vocal about the waves of support, reach outs and straight love she's received from those who have been in her position before: Lady Gaga, SZA, Ariana Grande, Charli XCX and Beyoncé, to name just a few. Pulling from the corners of country and folk too, Roan is the wonderful sum of all of her parts – a dash of Kate Bush, a sprinkle of Kacey Musgraves, Charli's punk spirit with Sabrina's flirtation, Gaga's ambition and Lorde's creative vision.

So speaking to any femmes out there, this world can sometimes make you feel like in order to be taken seriously, there are parts of yourself and your identity that have to be hardened or dampened down to get ahead. As if you can't be too into makeup or clothes or driven by raw, intense feelings without being written off as hysterical. Take from Chappell that those aspects of you can be precisely what makes you sing (literally and figuratively). Harness the power of your own version of girlhood and you can be the best version of yourself not only for you, but in a way that inspires others to be themselves too. There's so much rich culture and value in the work and art that women have made and continue to make and the last few years have been an incredible example of that, with women in pop absolutely *dominating* the landscape – and doing so with overwhelming innovation and positivity too.

'I just go back to that version of myself 'cause it is when I felt the most happy. I was free. And I just loved it. The dress-up part, [the] pretend part, the art, making and sewing little things, taking photos. That was my favourite part of my childhood. And so that's kind of what I'm recreating with this project. So it's from inner child work.'

A Chappell Education Playlist

'HELP ME' BY JONI MITCHELL

Joni Mitchell is one of the great romantic poets and this track is one of the best exhibits of that. It's a lilting confessional about the rough and tumble of falling in love, even when the subject of your love is withholding or imperfect. It's intoxicating, vulnerable and oh so charming, just like Chappell.

'WUTHERING HEIGHTS' BY KATE BUSH

Probably the most mentioned of all the lovely entries here, 'Wuthering Heights' is as campy as it gets. In a flowing red dress and matching tights, performing contemporary dance on the foggy moors, yelling for one of Emily Brontë's fictional characters Heathcliff from the perspective of another one, that's also a ghost. Yes, you read that correctly. The lead single from her debut album, Bush's track spent 4 weeks at the top of the UK charts and made her the first ever woman to get a No.1 single with a completely original song. Even more unbelievable when you learn that she wrote it at just 18 years old. A staggering feat!

'I HATE MYSELF FOR LOVING YOU' BY JOAN JETT & THE BLACKHEARTS

Chappell once said on a podcast with Drew Afualo that for a split second while watching Joan Jett performing she 'got fan culture'. The magnetic pull of watching women shred on guitars is a magical phenomenon and this song encapsulates that miracle so well, with a signature sprinkle of Chappell's own romantic pessimism too.'

'DREAMS' BY FLEETWOOD MAC

Stevie Nicks is one of the greatest songwriters of multiple generations and this track is a testament to that. Written in 10 minutes by her amid all the romantic disentanglements happening in the group at the time, the result is one of the most cinematic break-up songs in history. Melancholic and liberating, hopeful and nostalgic, conceptual and hyper-specific. With a viral mashup of 'Dreams' and 'Good Luck, Babe!' going viral on TikTok and Roan covering the song on her YouTube channel back in the day, this had to make the list.

'DANCING ON MY OWN' BY ROBYN

Another of the best breakup songs ever written, we've skipped forward a couple of decades and we're also in the club. The heartbreak, the pleading, the re signation, all soundtracked by a glitchy, ragged electro production is a lethal concoction. Chappell loves this song, I love this song, if you don't love this song, I'm a little worried for you honestly.

'MARINERS APARTMENT COMPLEX' BY LANA DEL REY

A huge inspiration and emotional companion for Chappell Roan, there is no Chappell education playlist without Lana Del Rey. Singing Lana songs is even nodded to in her own song 'Naked in Manhattan', and this is one of the tracks she's referring to.

'STAY' BY RIHANNA

A well-documented Riri fan, 'Stay' is a mainstay from the catalogue for the emo baddies among us. And a clip of Chappell covering it at the age of 15 corroborates that theory. It's pure, it's raw, it's all heart and rasp. There's not much else to say about it.

'COOL FOR THE SUMMER' BY DEMI LOVATO
Shouted out in an interview when Chappell was asked about songs she wishes she wrote, this rogue pick is kind of a sneak guilty pleasure. You couldn't walk five feet in 2015 without hearing it and once you did, rest assured you'll be humming it under your breath for the next 8 to 10 business days. You're welcome.

'34+35' BY ARIANA GRANDE
Chappell has been vocal about her love of pop princess Ariana throughout her rise, even sharing that she was her number one streamed artist of 2024. Taking it all the way back to her YouTube cover days, this sultry single from her 2020 album Positions is one that Roan graced with her very own rendition.

'LUCKY' BY BRITNEY SPEARS
It's no secret that Chappell likes to channel the spirit of Britney in her popstar moments on stage. But this song in particular ties in perfectly to the tensions Chappell has openly discussed of grappling with fortune and celebrity culture in this modern world.

9

ACTIVISM & COMMUNITY

'PEOPLE THINK EVERYONE IN THE MIDWEST AGREES WITH A FAR-RIGHT VIEWPOINT AND IT'S JUST NOT TRUE.'

This is it. That's right. We're going to talk about it. Politics. If you rolled your eyes or tried to skip ahead just now, know that both me and Chappell are judging you, just a little bit. But you're back here now and at the end of the day, that's all that counts.

Chappell has always been pretty clear that she's here for the girls, gays and theys. And she makes sure to stand on that business with her personal politics too, even when it means she'll face criticism. Alongside constantly shouting out and spotlighting the role that drag queens and gay clubs played in her early self-realisation, on tour, Roan invites local drag queens to open her shows, even doing the work to source queens internationally for her London and Manchester shows, for example. A portion of her tour profits have also been dedicated to For The Gworls, a Black Trans charity based out of New York. These are just two small symbols of intentional representation that give a platform to the cultures and communities that have inspired her most, in a way that *actually* makes a change.

Beyond that she's found ways to divert and leverage her pop culture fanbase for good, championing platforms like Propeller that direct traffic towards the causes you want to propel. On her profile, she's been propelling issues of reproductive freedom and LGBTQIA+ rights, and the site incentivises donations with an offering of unique experiences and rewards that you're in with a chance of winning, the more you give. There's even a leaderboard celebrating those racking up the most points. It's such a simple way to ask people to put their money where their mouth is at a time when these marginalised groups need it most. Her fans have shown up in their tens of thousands and raised almost $200,000 as of last summer alone.

At the Governor's Ball, while dressed as the very symbol of American freedom, Lady Liberty, Roan took it a step further and spoke out to remind people of the values that are inscribed on the statue itself. She called for freedom in trans rights, women's rights and all those oppressed in occupied territories. During the speech, she was visibly emotional and was met with roaring applause. Of that moment, that went viral, in her interview with Bowen Yang in *Interview Magazine*, Chappell admitted it was intimidating:

'It was hard to be like, "I'm going to say something that a lot of my family is going to be like, 'Wow, you crossed the line.'" It's emotional because I believe what I said, and what's sad is that me believing in who I am, and what I stand for, rubs against a lot of my home.'

And it wasn't the only time Roan has had to take such a public and overtly political stance, either. The US 2024 election proved to be another point of contention, with the star receiving backlash from both ends of the political spectrum for refusing to endorse either presidential candidate. With many dubbing her 'privileged' and accusing her of being out of touch, attempting to pressure her into backing the Democrats despite their own neglect on the issues she's been vocal about, like trans rights and the war on Gaza. Being clear about the faults with both candidates was ironically the most politically consistent stance Roan could have taken – especially given she was referring only to endorsing candidates not voting in general – but the 'lesser of two evils' narrative and political tension at the time meant that she was still vilified for not towing the party line.

It's often in these moments of truly hard decisions and diminishing returns that our activism and commitment to our communities is challenged. It's fairly obvious that the people who are fans of Chappell Roan are extremely unlikely to be Trump supporters, and so making the choice to stand firm in demanding more from politicians, in a moment where so many chose to settle, is a decision that carries limited risk but speaks a lot to Chappell's character. When so many public figures have been scared into silence on political issues that have fractured the veneer of global democracy, here is someone at the height of their ascent still unafraid to say the hard thing. And so whether it's all fun and games at a Chappell show, where fans are able to revel in the joy and play of queer culture and watch a queer woman exist as her fullest self, or in lively debate about the fate of a nation and a democracy, activism and community are pillars at the core of Chappell Roan's mission. A testament to the fact that it really doesn't have to be career over everything, sometimes we have to make the calls that we know we can actually live with, whether it comes with glory or not.

'I can't read my DMs anymore, because I cry so much, but when people are like, "Whatever you're doing, it helped me" – I don't think any award or any money or whatever can be exchanged for that compliment. I don't care about anything else, except giving space to people to be free. Because that's what I needed so bad: freedom.'

10

JOURNALLING

'WHENEVER I WAS IN THE MUSIC CAMPS, I LEARNED HOW TO WRITE SONGS. I FELT IT WAS THE FIRST TIME I'D EVER BEEN AROUND CREATIVE KIDS. LIKE, TRULY PEOPLE WHO WERE PASSIONATE ABOUT WRITING POEMS AND BEING EMOTIONAL. I JUST DIDN'T HAVE THAT GROWING UP.'

Journalling is an incredible tool for working through feelings you may not have spoken out loud yet, as well as a way to visualise and motivate things you dream of for your own future. At first it can feel a little unnatural, but the more you jump in and do it, the smoother it flows and the clearer your head starts to feel. You'd be amazed at how many times I've felt the overwhelming urge to crash out over text, or worse on social media, but instead I put pen to paper in my journal and magically feel cured. Taking even 10 minutes out of your day – especially as part of a relaxed morning routine – can do absolute wonders for your energy, momentum and emotional regulation. In fact, here are 10 ways that journalling regularly can drastically improve your life:

1. **Mental Clarity** – Providing a space for you to clear your mental clutter is so valuable in a world that can be so overstimulating and busy. Using it as a way to work through the thoughts that we may not feel ready to express out loud with friends and family can unknowingly bring us a lot closer to a conclusion. Something about writing things down rather than processing them inside your own head allows you to view a problem from a fresh perspective altogether. Better decision-making, fewer headaches, more efficient conflict resolution!

2. **Stress Reduction** – The emotional release alone cannot be overstated, even in cases where it doesn't necessarily feel like there's a problem to solve. Sometimes a journal session just feels like a deep, emotional offloading with a friend, without the baggage of having to worry about what you've just shared or if you've talked too much or wanting to take something back.

3. **Self-awareness** – Journallling encourages a level of reflection that we don't tend to make enough room for in our fast-paced lives. To take accountability in a way that doesn't feel loaded or even to leave questions that we don't yet have the answer to. One of the trippiest parts of journalling can also be time-travelling back through other periods of your life through your own journal entries and realising just how much the feelings you thought you'd never get past are so far in the rearview mirror now. It's a rare insight into our own growth and a powerful tool for self-discovery.

4. **Creative Boost** – Again, the act of free-flowing communication is an incredible way to generate new ideas that feels safe and not at all embarrassing. No two journals have to look the same, either; yours could take the form of mostly scribbles or bullet points while someone else's looks like poems or letters to self. The possibilities are very much endless and it's a totally

low-stakes way to trial any new methods or mediums you've been curious about, too.

5. **Communication Skills** – Journalling is such a gift for communication because it not only allows you to articulate your thoughts and feelings on your own before you bring them to others, but it's also a space to reflect and learn from the interactions you're already having. Seeing certain points written down on a page can be super useful in identifying misunderstandings and crossed wires, as well as things you might just want to correct or expand on.

6. **Emotional Processing** – Over time, being able to reflect on the things that happen to you not just as an instant release but to encourage a process of healing and learning is another way that journalling can be key, especially when it comes to areas of trauma and closure. It's a way to practise self-compassion and to voice the things that are most difficult to voice without fear of judgement and consequence.

7. **Gratitude Gardening** – I know this one feels a little cliché but you would be surprised just how effective a mood boost it can be to force yourself to list a few things in a day that you are thankful for. We so often treat our good fortune as a given, but taking a second

to sit in the positive can bring so much perspective and much-needed good, for want of a better word, back to the forefront of our lives.

8. **Memory and Retention** – Not to be all old man screaming at the sky again, but we don't write enough and it shows! Our attention spans and our memory are in the gutter and the very act of writing, the old-fashioned way, is just a small habit we can try to maintain that will help to address that. It's proven to nurture our memory and comprehension as well as just allowing us to better process, retain and utilise the information in our heads.

9. **Goal-setting** – What better way to set goals than with journalling? Speaking them into existence is all well and good but nothing quite beats the pressure of looking at last year's new year's resolutions and realising you've achieved none of them. WHICH IS ... FINE! But also chop chop.

10. **Sleep** – The last one is super simple, writing before bed and getting off your phone is just a sweet way to wind down and switch your brain off slowly. It clears racing thoughts and does not contain any blue light.

Prompts

If you're feeling stuck on what exactly to write about, but want to pick up the habit for self-betterment, here are some easy prompts to get you started.

If you woke up tomorrow and money as a concept didn't exist anymore, everything you needed was free – how would you want to spend your days?

Write a descriptive Day in the Life of a version of you 10 years from now who's living your dream life. Spare no details – add what you had for breakfast, what you're wearing, any evening plans, who's texting you, are you rocking a new hairstyle?

If you could move to any city in the world to pursue your dream, where would you go and why?

What's stopping you from working towards that in the next five years or so?

What's something that you'd love to shout from the rooftops if nobody you know could hear?

What are you proud of now that the version of you five years ago would not have been able to predict?

What's something you want to be proud of yourself for in five years' time that right now feels impossible?

Try to recall a stand-out positive memory this year. Describe it in detail, then unpack what made it so significant. What would you like to take from it and repeat regularly? How can you make that happen?

What's one thing you did just for yourself today?

Write down 10 things that you're proud of yourself for this week – big or small.

What's one thing you can do today to make someone in your community smile?

If you had to create your own alter ego, who could do and be anything, what would they be called, what would their talents be and how would they act?

Write a letter to yourself from the perspective of an old, wrinkly you 50 years in the future?

If your life was a movie, what film would it be and why?

What's something that you can do today, to help you feel ready for your dream, whenever it comes?

Think of a question or problem that you've been worrying about recently. Write about what the best-case scenario would be. Describe in detail the possible ways in which it actually might work out for the better and exceed your expectations.

11

QUIZ TIME

Which Chappell Song Are You?

1. How would you describe your energy at a party?

a. Life of the party – I'm almost certainly somewhere doing too much.

b. If the vibe is right, I'm having a good time, but if not I might pull a French exit.

c. A bit of a wild card. Even I don't know what energy I'm arriving with half the time.

2. What are you like when you're in a relationship?

a. I love hard and fast and openly. I'm all about owning my feelings, whatever they might be.

b. I've learned to keep my distance and protect my heart, but I'm not afraid to show love when it's real.

c. I like love to feel like an adventure. I want things to feel spontaneous and exciting.

3. Ideal night out?

a. A flashy, over-the-top event where everyone is dressed to impress and the energy is electric.

b. A chill gathering with close friends at a cosy spot, just vibing and enjoying each other's company.

c. A wild, carefree night where nothing is planned, and we're living in the moment. The night is ours to make anything happen.

4. Imagine you're feeling stressed out. What's your first go-to coping mechanism?

a. Take a minute, then do something that's out of my comfort zone to shake me out of it.

b. Take some time to myself, reflect and wait for things to become clearer.

c. I don't really get stressed but if I was, I'd probably just ride it out and lean into the chaos.

5. How would your best friends describe your style?

a. Fierce and unapologetically unique.

b. Chill, comfortable and effortlessly stylish.

c. Bold, experimental and always one step ahead.

6. Which of these best describes your life philosophy?

a. Be unforgettable.

b. Tell the truth, always.

c. Chase the unknown and embrace the unexpected.

7. What's your idea of success?

a. Being loud, proud and completely yourself, even in the face of those who doubt me.

b. Finding peace with myself and the people around me, no matter what the world throws at us.

c. Being bold, breaking barriers and doing things that make people stop and think, even if it ruffles some feathers.

8. What would the name of your memoir be?

a. *Living Out Loud*
b. *Only Time Will Tell*
c. *Young Heart, Run Free*

RESULTS

Mostly As:
You're 'Pink Pony Club'!
Even if you grew up in a small pond, you're absolutely a big fish – a showstopper, always the centre of attention, living life with boldness and flair. Like 'Pink Pony Club', you embrace your quirks and own your individuality, no matter what anyone else thinks. You're not afraid to step into the spotlight and express your true self – fun, fearless and unapologetically you!

Mostly Bs:
You're 'Good Luck, Babe'!
You've learned the art of balance and self-care. Like 'Good Luck, Babe!', you're a mix of vulnerability and strength. Grounded in reality but comfortable living in your own truth, you're not afraid to let your feelings lead and find yourself open to fun and connection. Whether that gets you hurt or sets you on your destined path, in your eyes, there's nothing more important than being honest and open with those you love.

Mostly Cs:
You're 'HOT TO GO!'
You live for the thrill and excitement of life. Like 'HOT TO GO!' you crave adventure, unpredictability and breaking free from the mundane constraints of the day-to-day. You're always ready to take risks, make bold moves and explore the unknown with reckless abandon. Your energy is infectious and you refuse to play by the rules, inspiring others around you to do the same.

A Song For Every Occasion

When you're headed out out ...
'After Midnight'
Inspired by a phrase Chappell was always told by her parents, that 'nothing good happens after midnight', this track is an embrace of the opposite. Leaning into the twinkling magic and possibilities of the night, it's a disco-infused bop about throwing away the rulebook and chasing fun for once. It's the definition of good, flirty fun!

When you just got dumped ...
'Casual'
Impossible to listen to at any volume level other than maximum, this is the belt-your-heart-out ballad about the frustrations of loving someone who can't (or worse, won't) give you what you need. Equal parts fury and nostalgia, this is the song for you when you're in the anger stage of grieving a situationship. Even though it's vulnerable and full of pain, there's something freeing about the biting sarcasm of it and the receipts Chappell lists as the song progresses.

When you want revenge ...
'My Kink Is Karma'
This is the perfect song to soundtrack a step into your inner villain era. In general we strive to be good people but we have to allow ourselves a little wriggle room every now and then. After all, how can we really enjoy the sweet moments in life if we never get the chance to be a little salty?

When you told them so ...
'Good Luck, Babe!'
In a similar vein, this anthem is all about letting the chips fall where they may, even when you hate the hand you're dealt. A dabble into the world of bitterness is all well and good but ultimately, the real comfort is when you know that you know better and are sure that time will tell. In the words of Kylie Jenner, not everyone can have the privilege of realising things on the same schedule as you. And if you're ahead of the curve, clued up, sometimes life can feel like a waiting game. In the meantime, relish the knowledge that you were right all along.

When you're feeling yourself ...
'HOT TO GO!'
This song is drunk on desire. For fleeting moments, falling in love with strangers on the dance floor and being totally, completely unashamed in going after what you want when you want it. Because what's the worst that could happen? If you're feeling yourself in the mirror in your bedroom or if you need that burst of energy before a big date, this is the one for you.

When you're feeling lost ...
'California'
One of the earliest songs on her album, 'California' was written at a point when Chappell was feeling sad in Los Angeles before she had even moved back to Missouri. Exploring that moment when you take a leap of faith or a step towards what you think you should be. A place that makes you happy, expecting it to fit like a glove but realising it might take longer and be much harder than you thought it would be. This is a ballad for the homesick, the existential, the questioning.

When you're feeling brave, bold and beautiful ...
'Super Graphic Ultra Modern Girl'
This is a club tune for the baddies who aren't afraid to be themselves, regardless of what anyone else thinks about it. Ironically inspired by an *Architectural Digest* video that Chappell watched, where someone was describing an interior design choice, this track can kind of mean whatever you want it to mean, and that's the beauty of it. What does super graphic mean to you? How can you bring an ultra-modern edge into your life?

When you're following your dreams ...
'Pink Pony Club'
This song tells a story. It has drama, longing and an infectious kind of strength. Play this when you need that little boost of assurance that everything is going to be okay, even when it feels like that isn't guaranteed. Sometimes our heart pulls us towards purposes so much bigger than ourselves and there's no greater testament to that than this track, its message and the role it played within Chappell's own ascent to stardom.

How Femininomenal Are You?

Answer the following questions to determine just how femininomenal you are ...

1. How would your best friend describe you in one word?
. Chill (1)
. Quirky (2)
. Unapologetic (3)

2. When you're relaxing after a long day, you go to put on ...
. 'Cool For The Summer' by Demi Lovato (3)
. 'Taste' by Sabrina Carpenter (2)
. '360' by Charli XCX (1)

3. You're going on a first date, what's the outfit vibe?
. Jeans and a nice top (1)
. Pink tank top, bedazzled cargo shorts and cowboy boots (2)
. A fully-fledged vintage mermaid costume (3)

4. Someone you don't know asks you for a hug, what do you do?
. Give them a hug! (1)
. Absolutely not (3)
. Offer a high five instead (2)

5. What do you look for in a partner?
. Something casual, no pressure (1)
. I need to be obsessed (3)
. Strong and stable (2)

6. Go-to Netflix and chill pick?
. *Bottoms* (3)
. *The Worst Person in the World* (2)
. *Everything Now* (1)

7. Who would be your celebrity best friend?
. Bowen Yang (1)
. Ariana Grande (2)
. Julia Fox (3)

8. One thing you'd change in the world if you could?
. Eat the rich (2)
. Let everyone love who they want to love (3)
. Reverse climate change (1)

9. What's your dream place to live?
. 50/50 split between a 1920s villa in West Hollywood
  and a secluded lake house (3)
. A New York loft apartment (2)
. A sprawling country manor (1)

10. If you weren't a world-famous pop star, you'd be ...
. A kindergarten teacher (1)
. Something in genetics (3)
. A despondent speciality barista (2)

RESULTS

0-10 Great effort. When it comes to your journey as a Midwest Princess, you are very much still in the rise part – navigating through the ups and downs to find yourself. But rest assured! You will get there. Your vision is forming and your talents know no bounds, it's just a matter of time before it all comes together.

10-20 Well done, babe! You are well on your way to superstardom. You're guided by your instincts and, heck, most of the time they are 100 per cent spot on. With a little more time and a lot more glitter, you should be femininomenal in no time at all.

20-30: Chappell, is that you? Congratulations! You are a veritable Red Wine Supernova – you shine so brightly that the rest of us might need sunglasses to bear witness. Reaching icon status is like breathing to you, it comes so easy. You're a magnificent bag of contradictions: glamorous and chaotic, earthy and haute couture, a sensitive soul that takes no prisoners.

How Well Do You Know Chappell?

1. In what year was Chappell born?
a. 1998
b. 1996
c. 2000
d. 2001

2. Where was she born?
a. Willard, Missouri
b. Abilene, Kansas
c. Holland, Michigan
d. Gallena, Illinois

3. What's her real first name?
a. Katherine
b. Kayleigh
c. Kylie
d. Kristina-Michelle

4. What is the colour of the club that Chappell sings about dancing at?
a. Blue
b. Purple
c. Pink
d. Green

5. Chappell's fame skyrocketed while supporting which artist on their tour?

a. Sabrina Carpenter

b. Olivia Rodrigo

c. Billie Eilish

d. Charli XCX

6. Which celebrity covered Chappell's hit single 'Good Luck, Babe!' on BBC Radio 1 Live Lounge, as well as while touring?

a. Sabrina Carpenter

b. Olivia Rodrigo

c. Billie Eilish

d. Charli XCX

7. What object did Chappell credit for her big wig during her performance at NPR's Tiny Desk Concert?

a. Newspaper

b. Tights

c. Bubble wrap

d. Trash bag

8. Which of these jobs did Chappell not have?

a. Summer camp counsellor

b. Barista

c. Wedding singer

d. Nanny

9. Which of these star signs do not appear in Chappell's astrological big three?

a. Leo
b. Pisces
c. Sagittarius
d. Libra

10. Which drag queen inspired her famous catchphrase: 'your favourite artist's favourite artist'?

a. Bimini Bon Boulash
b. Plane Jane
c. Divine
d. Sasha Colby

ANSWERS

1A 2A 3B 4C 5B 6A 7D 8C 9A 10D

References

INTRODUCTION – 10 YEARS IN THE MAKING

'Chappell Roan on The Rise and Fall of a Midwest Princess, perseverance and the freedom of drag', *Q with Tom Power,* 19 Oct 2023. (https://www.youtube.com/watch?v=f5UBV_Gpihg)

'Chappell Roan Talks Outfit Inspirations, New Album and Your Favorite Artist's Favorite Artist', *The Tonight Show Starring Jimmy Fallon*, 21 Jun 2024. (https://www.youtube.com/watch?v=L94zTNhLnXo)

'Chappell Roan on being busy and glamorous & why 'Good Luck, Babe!' inspires her (Interview)', *Triple J.* 8 Jun 2024. (https://www.youtube.com/watch?v=jTYKJkXkDel&t=312s)

MIDWEST PRINCESS

'Chappell Roan – The Rise and Fall of a Midwest Princess (Episode 1: Homecoming)'. *Chappell Roan,* 16 Aug 2023. (https://www.youtube.com/watch?v=xR55tlcWNVg)

'Chappell Roan on Queer Music, the Midwest, and Olivia Rodrigo', *TIME,* 1 Mar 2024. (https://www.youtube.com/watch?v=6Qv8MySbN-o)

PINK PONY CLUB

Cai, Delia. 'The femininomenonal ascent of Chappell Roan', *The Face,* 16 Sep 2024. (https://theface.com/music/chappell-roan-pop-music-famous-interview-good-luck-babe)

Fromson, Audrey. 'Chappell Roan on Making Pop Music and Giving Back', *Vanity Fair,* 18 Sep 2023. (https://www.vanityfair.com/style/2023/09/chappell-roan-on-making-pop-music-and-giving-back?srsltid=AfmBOoo8ZewLqc9LX760B1CxBnFHJxmgT6Gx4K-ATKn_G4KqFJROBmVq)

Kaplan, Ilana. 'Chappell Roan on Her Love of Drag Queens and Her Debut Album That 'Feels Like a Party' (Exclusive)', *People,* 27 Sep 2023. (https://people.com/chappell-roan-new-album-rise-fall-midwest princess-exclusive-7974688)

Solomon, Kate. 'Fame is like going through puberty': Chappell Roan on sexuality, superstardom and the joy of drag', *Guardian,* 20 Sep 2024. (https://www.theguardian.com/music/2024/sep/20/fame-is-like-going-through-puberty-chappell-roan-on-sexuality-superstardom-and-the-joy-of-drag)

HOW TO BE AUTHENTICALLY YOU

Arabi, Shahida. 'Do You Seek Validation from Others? Here's How to Stop', *Psych Central,* 30 Mar 2022. (https://psychcentral.com/health/steps-to-stop-seeking-approval-from-others)

Fromson, Audrey. 'Chappell Roan on Making Pop Music and Giving Back', *Vanity Fair,* 18 Sep 2023. (https://www.vanityfair.com/style/2023/09/chappell-roan-on-making-pop-music-and-giving-back?srsltid=AfmBOoo8ZewLqc9LX760B1CxBnFHJxmgT6Gx4K-ATKn_G4KqFJROBmVq)

Yang, Bowen. 'Chappell Roan and Bowen Yang on Queers, Fears, and Surviving Superstardom', *Interview Magazine*, 19 Aug 2024. (https://www.interviewmagazine.com/music/chappell-roan-and-bowen-yang-on-queers-fears-and-surviving-superstardom)

LOVER GWORL
Carter, Ashleigh. 'Chappell Roan Opens Up About Falling in Love, Rise to Fame, and More', *Teen Vogue*, 10 Nov 2024. (https://www.teenvogue.com/story/chappell-roan-grammy-museum-interview)
Specter, Emma. 'What Is Limerence, The Not-So-Desirable Dating Trend Du Jour?', *Vogue*, 17 Apr 2024. (https://www.vogue.co.uk/article/limerance)
Yang, Bowen. 'Chappell Roan and Bowen Yang on Queers, Fears, and Surviving Superstardom', *Interview Magazine*, 19 Aug 2024. (https://www.interviewmagazine.com/music/chappell-roan-and-bowen-yang-on-queers-fears-and-surviving-superstardom)

CAMP ROAN!
@1800andrewdahling, Instagram, November 2024
@raisaflowers, Instagram, November 2024
@isamayaffrench, Instagram, November 2024
@leana.ardeleanu, Instagram, November 2024
@naezrahlooks, Instagram, November 2024
'Chappell Roan – The Rise and Fall of a Midwest Princess (Episode 1: Homecoming)'. *Chappell Roan*. 16 Aug 2023. (https://www.youtube.com/watch?v=xR55tlcWNVg)
'Chappell Roan – The Rise and Fall of a Midwest Princess (Episode 2: Dream Come True)'. *Chappell Roan*. 5 Sept 2023. (https://www.youtube.com/watch?v=pTRzTGP6P0Q)
'Chappell Roan Breaks Down Every Song On "The Rise and Fall of a Midwest Princess" | Making The Album', *Capital Buzz*. 16 Jan 2024. (https://www.youtube.com/watch?v=PF96UOulHw0)
'Chappell Roan Talks Outfit Inspirations, New Album and Your Favorite Artist's Favorite Artist'. *The Tonight Show Starring Jimmy Fallon*, 21 Jun 2024. (https://www.youtube.com/watch?v=L94zTNhLnXo)
Atlanta, Ellen. 'An ode to Chappell Roan's make-up, the hottest thing in beauty right now', *Dazed*, 11 Jul 2024. (https://www.dazeddigital.com/beauty/article/63067/1/an-ode-to-chappell-roan-s-make-up-beauty-ellen-atlanta-divine)
Fromson, Audrey. 'Chappell Roan on Making Pop Music and Giving Back', Vanity Fair, 18 Sep 2023. (https://www.vanityfair.com/style/2023/09/chappell-roan-on-making-pop-music-and-giving-back?srsltid=AfmBOoo8ZewLqc9LX760B1CxBnFHJxmgT6Gx4K-ATKn_G4KqFJROBmVq)

Jackson, Hannah. 'Genesis Webb Is More Than Chappell Roan's Stylist', *Vogue,* 3 July 2024. (https://www.vogue.co.uk/article/chappell-roan-stylist-genesis-webb)

Kirilenko, Calissa. 'TikTok's "Dopamine Menu" Is a Game-Changer–Here's How to Make Your Own', *The Every Girl,* 29 Aug 2024. (https://theeverygirl.com/dopamine-menu-to-boost-mood/)

Neagen, Ally. 'TikTok's dopamine menu trend explained, and how to curate yours', *Glamour UK,* 2 Sept 2024. (https://www.glamourmagazine.co.uk/article/dopamine-menu-trend-tiktok)

Summers, Joan. 'Chappell Roan Is Taking It', *Paper Mag,* 4 Jun 2024. (https://www.papermag.com/chappell-roan-trixie-mattel#rebelltitem22)

LET'S TALK ABOUT BOUNDARIES

Pattemore, Chantelle. '10 Ways to Build and Preserve Better Boundaries', *PsychCentral,* 3 Jun 2021. (https://psychcentral.com/lib/10-way-to-build-and-preserve-better-boundaries)

Reid, Sheldon. 'Setting Healthy Boundaries In Relationships', *HelpGuide.org,* 30 Nov 2024. (https://www.helpguide.org/relationships/social-connection/setting-healthy-boundaries-in-relationships)

Solomon, Kate. ''Fame is like going through puberty': Chappell Roan on sexuality, superstardom and the joy of drag', *The Guardian,* 20 Sep 2024. (https://www.theguardian.com/music/2024/sep/20/fame-is-like-going-through-puberty-chappell-roan-on-sexuality-superstardom-and-the-joy-of-drag)

@chappellroan, TikTok, November 2024

A PHENOMENON OF THE FEMME VARIETY

'Chappell Roan on The Rise and Fall of a Midwest Princess, perseverance and the freedom of drag'. *Q with Tom Power.* 19 Oct 2023. (https://www.youtube.com/watch?v=f5UBV_Gpihg)

'The artists Chappell fangirls over | The Comment Section with Drew Afualo', *Spotify.* 19 Jul 2024. (https://www.youtube.com/watch?v=z0EckAyVuJc)

'Chappell Roan Breaks Down Every Song On "The Rise and Fall of a Midwest Princess" | Making The Album', *Capital Buzz.* 16 Jan 2024. (https://www.youtube.com/watch?v=PF96UOuIHw0)

Fromson, Audrey. 'Chappell Roan on Making Pop Music and Giving Back', *Vanity Fair,* 18 Sep 2023. (https://www.vanityfair.com/style/2023/09/chappell-roan-on-making-pop-music-and-giving-back?srsltid=AfmBOoo8ZewLqc9LX760B1CxBnFHJxmgT6Gx4K-ATKn_G4KqFJROBmVq)

ACTIVISM & COMMUNITY

'Chappell Roan on being busy and glamorous & why "Good Luck, Babe!" inspires her (Interview)'. *Triple J.* 8 Jun 2024. (https://www.youtube.com/watch?v=jTYKJkXkDeI&t=312s)

Cai, Delia. 'The femininomenonal ascent of Chappell Roan', *The Face*, 16 Sep 2024. (https://theface.com/music/chappell-roan-pop-music-famous-interview-good-luck-babe)

Yang, Bowen. 'Chappell Roan and Bowen Yang on Queers, Fears, and Surviving Superstardom', *Interview Magazine*, 19 Aug 2024. (https://www.interviewmagazine.com/music/chappell-roan-and-bowen-yang-on-queers-fears-and-surviving-superstardom)

JOURNALLING

Fromson, Audrey. 'Chappell Roan on Making Pop Music and Giving Back', *Vanity Fair*, 18 Sep 2023. (https://www.vanityfair.com/style/2023/09/chappell-roan-on-making-pop-music-and-giving-back?srsltid=AfmBOoo8ZewLqc9LX760B1CxBnFHJxmgT6Gx4K-ATKn_G4KqFJROBmVq)

Phelan, Hayley. 'What's All This About Journaling?', *The New York Times*, 25 Oct 2018. (https://www.nytimes.com/2018/10/25/style/journaling-benefits.html)

Picture Credits

P4: Scott Kowalchyk/CBS via Getty Images
P6: Daniel DeSlover/ZUMA Press Wire/Shutterstock
P12,23,56: Jason Kempin/Getty Images
P14: Dana Jacobs/FilmMagic/Getty Images
P28, 120: Dania Maxwell/Los Angeles Times via Getty Images
P30: Michael Loccisano/Getty Images for MTV
P37, 70: Astrida Valigorsky/Getty Images
P38: Rick Kern/Getty Images
P43,96: Michael Hurcomb/Shutterstock
P46: Steve Jennings/FilmMagic/Getty Images
P60: Kristin Callahan/Shutterstock
P84: Larry Marano/Shutterstock
P90: Katja Ogrin/Redferns/Getty Images
P106: Timothy Hiatt/Shutterstock
P111: Gary Miller/FilmMagic/Getty Image
P114: Kevin Mazur/Getty Images for MTV/Getty Images
P124: Jim Dyson/Getty Images
P129: Matthew J. Lee/The Boston Globe via Getty Images
P137: Annie Lesser/imageSPACE/Shutterstock

All other images: Shutterstock.com